1

Episode ⌣⍳⍸

The Great Remembering

Scaliger seduced me: chronological studies, as I see, terrify me.

Ioannes Kepler

For those who will start with it, yes, time is an 'illusion.' In our case, it is also part of a Belief System, a belief system that has the power to enslave or even kill. Therefore saying time is an illusion does not help. Deeply manipulated linear time is one in a set of powerful weapons being used against us until we can set that aside. This is the story. As always, I think a story will help...and remember, one cannot know the truth without first knowing the lie.

What if every war, every altercation, every diaspora, every holocaust on record was simply part of one very long campaign....one and the same campaign...meant to wipe out the remnants of the greatest civilization this beautiful world has ever known, seeded likely by the Phe, from the constellation of Ursa Major, evidence of whom is indeed overwhelming and everywhere? What if the purpose of chemtrailing, schooling, the media, the vaccine program, fracking, the ruthless collecting up and bottling of the world's surface water supply, was to make damned sure all memory of what came before was eradicated? What if CERN and its recent calls for 'artistic types' was a desperation move to try to harness our Imagination to punch a hole into the morphogenic field, the material with which we project things we can touch, see, hear and feel on this planet? What if we are, in fact, only a few hundred years away from the survivors of the Atlantean civilization, a civilization which was a direct

2

result of the seeding of the Phe?

In the beginning, in the middle, in the end...it's all about why...once something is known or revealed or re-membered, then what? Well, I am not alone on this plane and neither are you. If I see it, I share it. And so, as Anatoly Fomenko and so many others have done, I try to collate and bring a broad stroke complete with resources so that the reader can go as deep as wanted. The idea is to share this information as far and wide as possible. If the Scaligerian Chronology, the one used as The Chronology 'Bible', has been proved false, then that should be known complete with the ample attendant verification from other scientists. If Fomenko and his team are trying to reconstruct what might be considered as close to a true chronology as possible, then that also must be shared far and wide: taught, if you will, as an antidote to the mass indoctrination we receive in 'schools.' I intend to be part of that.

Even if it's all an hologram, I'll create my own hologram, thank you very much. The organic kind, the authentic kind, the enlivened kind. I really am fed up with being robbed of the truth and, essentially, this sticky false chronology web has been spun around us to divert and subsequently steal and use our energy without our conscious consent and awareness. However, in order to keep us from coming to an honest realization based on the mathematical data in the heavens, we have been severed more and more from the sun and the stars in a completely artificial and toxic way. Just getting between us and the sun is crippling to us in many ways until our higher selves adjust and attenuate. Add to that all of the poisons and hard or soft or medium ware in the plasma now enveloping us which is meant also to block out the sunlight itself and we have slow boiling death for any entity that breathes...only at this point it's not so slow. This subject goes directly to the Aerosol War, Chemtrailing, and Geoengineering.

The currently accepted chronicle......the great lie.

	Book Text: Antiquity	Graphics from the World History Chart	blue words = links		
America	Peru : Chavin and Paracas cultures	Mexico : Olmec culture at its peak	Olmec ceremonial center at La Venta	La Venta destroyed by violence	
Italy	Villanova culture by Italic peoples (Iron Age)	Etruscan civilization in Italy	Legendary reign of seven kings over Rome	Etruscan league of twelve cities	Roman Republic evolves
Europe	Late Bronze Age	Druids in Gaul and Britain	Celtic tribes in Gaul (Early Iron Age)	Scythian tribes in Russia	
Greece	Dorian migration	Iliad & Odyssey composed — Greek Colonization (Magna Graecia)	Reform of Cleisthenes	Athenian Empire	
	Greek settlements in Ionia (Miletus)	Growth of Greek city states (Polis) — Rise of Sparta — Tyranny of Corinth	Reform of Solon — Law Code of Dracon	Tyranny of Peisistratus — Classical Age	
	Olympic Games — Messenian War — Republic founded in Athens			Persian Wars	
Asia Minor	Semitic-speaking Arameans from Arabia rule over Mesopotamia	NEW ASSYRIAN EMPIRE (cap. Nineveh)	MEDIA (cap. Ecbatana)	Persia conquers Media	PERSIA (cap. Persepolis)
	Phoenicia (cap. Tyre) — Control of Mediterranean trade — Carthage founded in N'Africa	Assyrian world domination — Conquests of Babylon, Syria and Palestine	BABYLONIA (New Babylonian Empire)	The Pers. empire was the first major indo-European power	Greek Campaigns
	Hebrews unite Judah and Israel — King David — Israel (cap. Samaria) Elijah and Elisha	Impalement used to subject conquered peoples — Kdm divided Judah (cap. Jerusalem)	Isaiah appears — Judah pays tribute to Assyria	Jews in Babyl. captivity	
Egypt	The New Kdm	The declining kdm split into Middle Egypt ruled by priests at Thebes and into Lower Egypt dominated by Lybians	Egypt ruled by Nubia — Psamtik frees Egypt from foreign rule — Egypt becomes a sea power		Egypt becomes part of the Persian empire
	–1000	–900	–800	–700	–600	–500
India	Rig Veda (from ca.1500 BC) — Caste system evolves	EPIC AGE — The two Epics the 'Mahabharata' and the 'Ramayana' relate to events of the epic age	Upanishads and Brahmanas composed	Republics evolve along the Himalayas	N'West India part of Persian emp. — dominates the Ganges area
China	to text Chou — Western CHOU (cap. Hao) — The kings land surrounded by small feudal states. Central power could not expand, thus vassals grew strong & independent.	A Barbarian attack overwhelmed the old capital Hao and central authority declined	Eastern CHOU (cap. Lo-yang) — Spring and Autumn period	Age of philosophers	Division of China into separate states
Africa	Some priests from Egypt migrate to Nubia (Sudan) where they establish a theocratic state	Kush kdm conquers Nubia	Egyptian culture survives in the Kush kdm (cap. Meroe) in the Sudan		

The diversion and theft are orchestrated by Predatory Parasites who have, in effect, captured this planet for at least the past thousand years but likely far longer than that. It would be impossible to say necessarily how much longer than that although I imagine the answer could be approximated with close study of the 'ancient' oral histories such as the Vedic texts or the Bardic histories from Ireland. It doesn't matter nearly as much as understanding that this has actually happened. One could also say the orchestrated synthetic entity called the Prussian Aristocracy, or the 'people' behind it, have stolen every throne on the globe. It is also well-known that the Jesuit Order, by their own blatant admission, are the puppet masters behind each of these 'royal' lines, behind each political line, and behind each religious authority. Naturally, there is likely a non-earth parasite behind the Jesuits.

The following is an excerpt from the Oath of the Jesuits: *I furthermore promise and declare that I will, when opportunity present, make and wage relentless war, secretly or openly, against all heretics, Protestants and Liberals, as I am directed to do, to extirpate and exterminate them from the face of the whole earth; and that I will spare neither age, sex or condition; and that I will hang, waste, boil, flay, strangle and bury alive these infamous heretics, rip up the stomachs and wombs of their women and crush their infants' heads against the walls, in order to annihilate forever their execrable race. That when the same cannot be done openly, I will secretly use the poisoned cup, the strangulating cord, the steel of the poniard or the leaden bullet, regardless of the honor, rank, dignity, or authority of the person or persons, whatever may be their condition in life, either public or private, as I at any time may be directed so to do by any agent of the Pope or Superior of the Brotherhood of the Holy Faith, of the Society of Jesus.*

These, my friends, are the bad fairies.

I care not in this Episode which of those descriptions is the easiest with which to work. The reader should pick whatever works for them. The point is to really grasp how far this parasitic entity is willing to go. And why not? The Jesuit-run Prussian Parasite Pretender, Elizabeth of Saxe-Coburg-Gotha (Windsor), has enough real money, land holdings, and commodities to cure every housing and food problem on ten planets and yet she sits on it, hordes it, does god knows what with it in the wee hours of the night. And we let her get away with it!! The Jesuit-run Vatican has sequestered every means of artistic communication and symbolism it can get its pilfering hands on and stowed it all underneath the Vatican in what must amount to mile after mile of subterranean vaults. Whatever resources Lizzie doesn't already have, Petrus Romanus has. The rest of the world gets to split the three cents that's left over and blame each other for our misery. And we let them get away with it. We will visit that in depth in the Episode covering the Saviour Programming.

There are three or four primary delivery systems of the coercion apparatus used against us and each Episode delves very deeply into one of them. (Episode, by the way, is a literary term stolen by the television industry. I am reclaiming it). What I bring will not be exhaustive because this is a Workbook, which means it is a collaborative endeavour between the writer/researcher and the reader. However, it may be exhausting. It may challenge your ability to keep your cognitive dissonance hounds at bay in a profound way. Lucky for us, the evidence is based in sciences: maths and astronomy. These are sources of both proofs and mystery solving with which we are well-acquainted. These are trusted friends for many.

It has been suggested to me, and was also in relation to the first book in this series, that this material can and maybe ought to be serialized. I agree. I agree much more than I did with the first book because these chapters delve deep, plunging right down to the darkest bowels of our situation. They really are small explosive books of their own. And even the small explosive books may, in the end, be serialized, depending on how deeply it seems the subject needs to be explored. So the plan is to release each Episode as it is and then, of course, in the end there will be a complete Imagination Chronicles, Book Two, the Workbook. There will be a pertinent preamble, radical statement, and introduction to each Episode. They can be taken quite separately and should, in the end, be taken together.

For me, it all started when a van ran my mother down in the road and killed her. For you, maybe it all started with the white criss-crosses in the sky. Suddenly the sun was surrounded by a sulphuric haze. NASA began distributing educational materials showing 'new' kinds of clouds. People all over the globe began to report mysterious illnesses: mimicking heart attacks, and pulmonary distress and lingering coughs that seemed to have no cause became the third leading killer in the USA. Solar visibility was reduced by a minimum of twenty percent, Vitamin D became almost impossible to come by naturally. We knew it was a slow-boil eradication under way. But there were other agendas. It is by means of bio-photonic ingestion or processing that we sustain ourselves as humans. It is by means of spherical astronomical mathematics that we keep track of time. It is by means of predictable records of eclipses and comets and the like that we date events. It has become more and more clear that something is terribly wrong with the history of events, the chronology. Terribly wrong. If we cannot see the heavens and if accepted astronomy is discounted then the absolute proof of what has been done to us...poof...disappears. This is what the Flat Earth Theory has been rolled out to accomplish, in my estimation.

Some of what's wrong in a nutshell? It is quite likely that

everything we think we 'know' about ancient Greece, Egypt, and Rome was made up during the Renaissance. The so-called ancient city of Troy was located in Italy and fell just before Rome rose. Rome was quite likely begun by a son of Ulysses. Aeneas, Romulus and Remus never existed. All of this happened in the Middle Ages. Additionally the second Roman Empire and the Third Roman Empire were one and the same, the third laid right on top of the second. And, finally, those two periods were the identical incidents we came to know as the Kingdom of Jerusalem, also known as the medieval city of Constantinople, and the Kingdom of Judea. The usurper Prussian Emperor, Frederich II, erected and supported by the Teutonic Knights, had himself declared the King of Jerusalem. The bloody Jesuits were disbanded by Pope Clement XIV, who was immediately poisoned by them, and they were reinstated by Pope Pius X when he was released from a Napoleonic prison just before the establishment of the Prussian Education System. Jesus the Christ was a medieval figure born around 1053 AD. Chronologists, mathematicians, and astronomers since Isaac Newton have known this and said so. We are much closer to Atlantean survivors in time than we could possibly imagine. We will, quite rightly, discuss the who, what, where, when and why...although we have touched upon some of it already.

What: The last 1,000 years plus of what we think of as history is a lie. It is a complete fabrication drilled into us as we sit hostage in the indoctrination camps we call schools. What has been forgotten while all of this is going on is that there was a time, not so long ago, when none of it was going on. Furthermore, we knew it was a lie but we did not know it was a *LIE*.

From about 200 AD, the likely true date of the invasion by the Teutonic Knights, sent from Jerusalem by the Knights Templar to swallow the Germanic principalities whole and create the Prussian Empire, to the present moment, all dates and the histories associated with them have been contrived to enslave us. Wars (mostly), monarchies, migrations, plagues, colonialism, the rise of the Roman Catholics, the Classical Period, the Reformation and the Anti-Reformation...all of it nonsense aimed at us to spin our heads around while a few plundered our planet. Indigenous peoples, so connected to the music and rhythm of the planet and how to nurture her, were ruthlessly eradicated or nearly so. Whatever truth may have existed within each of these historical 'events' is only visible with a microscope. Most of it is simply false.

Now that we are drowning in the filth conjured up by the Parasites and Predators, the story of man as monster, we are going to remember that there is only one story. So says the famous **mythologist, Joseph Campbell; it is** *The Hero's Journey*. **It is the story of each one of us as we leave the habitual boredom of the vacuous known and venture into the unknown, to find there the Pearl of Great Price and bring it back into our everyday lives. And when we refuse to do this, we become ill. When we are kept off this path, which is an esoteric crime of a higher order than murder, we become ill. We are being kept well off the path.**

*W*e will remember and reclaim the very immediate history of **a glorious 'just-past' in which we are magical and mighty. It is a multi-layered situation. On the one hand, we are majestic creatures, rare and to be desired by other creatures, creatures who do not have what we have and who cannot do what we do. The current situation is the result of dedicated enemy activity aimed at us likely since before the Battle of the Boyne and the arrival of the archontic infection1 in the Middle East. In fact, these two events were likely right on top of each other. The Boyne is epic but not a true battle; rather it may have been a re-enactment of the arrival of an artificial intelligence of some sort to our planet. It may have been a re-enactment of the arrival of the Archontic Infection. No matter what, it was a Masonic Ritual, of the highest order, and so one can safely conclude that this geographical area must be one of**

---

1   http://www.metahistory.org/gnostique/archonfiles/AlienIntrusion.php John Lash on the Gnostic texts which describes the arrival and activity of the Archons.

8

the most powerful places on earth. **The Battle of the Boyne was simply meant to esoterically, and black-magically, hand the British Isles to William III, Prince of Orange who, as such, outranked King James of England. 2 There was an event which preceded the Battle of the Boyne, the Battle(s) of Moytura, which may actually describe the arrival of the Parasite.3 No matter what, the Battles of Moytura centre around the Phe and perhaps the two factions of the Phe (good and evil). Certainly, the Phe are present now as they would be.**

Generally speaking the choice of that site and the strength therein may well go directly to the location Heart(h) of the Celts, as it were. (As it were it may well be for the location of the Celtic Heart(h) I believe does not obey the laws of time and space. In fact, the location of such may be linked to the arrival of the Phe on this planet)**4. The date for this battle may precede the invasions of the Teutonic Knights or it could be the other way around. It all depends on when and where we decide the infection arrived, what the infection is, and what was already here when it did. We can do that after we get everything straightened out. Certainly the Knights Templar in and around Jerusalem were infected with what we might now call psychopathy. Or, better, the infection that leads to psychopathy...infectious psychopathy carefully safeguarded and hard-wired through selective in-breeding. This practice continues today among the royal houses globally.**

In the last 211 years (allegedly), since Napoleon defeated Prussia at Jena, the effort to conquer human consciousness has become much, much more strenuous and even more ruthless. This thwarted psychopathic ruler in concert with the bloodthirsty hounds called the Jesuits, hell bent on revenge

2   Power, Andrew. Ireland, Land of the Pharaohs. The River Boyne symbolizing the Galaxy.
     https://apollosolaris.files.wordpress.com/2014/10/irelandlandofthepharoa0hs.pdf

3   Frazer, J. *The Battle of Moytura: The First Battle of Mag Tuired* and/or
     https://www.youtube.com/watch?v=4WB17qv-joc

4   Landmann, Erhard. *Women of the Phe*

after Pope Clement XIV dissolved their organization5 recreated a form of ruthless mind-bending not seen since the Spartan camps created Death Warriors. It is hard to imagine that as possible but it is the case and continues to become deeper and more intense. With the help of this mechanism, the Prussian Education System, these Predatory Parasites have been able to effectively erase our short-term memory and detach us from our own power. (Thanks to the Folk Souls in the morphogenic field and our unseverable relationship with the same, we are coming back to consciousness)6. The Memory tries very hard to return over and over and so this is a constant battle between us and them. Water especially is a battleground as water holds Memory and we are mostly made of water. Water seeks its own level and Memory does, too. (Memory to me is a proper noun and so I will always treat it as such by capitalizing). Think of fracking and all that's happening to destroy the oceans. Think of CERN doing deep damage to the ley lines. Think of Fukushima's radioactive death flooding the Pacific Ocean and the ground water beneath that nuclear plant.

It is likely that survivors from Atlantis were alive on this planet everywhere, functioning, building, teaching, battling and periodically fleeing from the Predatory Parasite whose aim it was to eradicate them and their knowledge and abilities from the earth. Analysis of settlements and monuments and ancient cities reveal that these sites are not so ancient on the one hand and that they simply could not have been constructed by the people in the area if they were at the point of development often characterized in the legends.(source) Additionally, wars all over the planet, but most recently in the middle east and eastern Europe are directly aimed at destroying evidence of these peoples who were our very recent ancestors.7

"A lot of us are open to the idea that there was an ancient advanced culture...Atlantis and Hyperborea perhaps and maybe these Seeders

5   https://en.wikipedia.org/wiki/Suppression_of_the_Society_of_Jesus
6   St.Louis, C. *Dangerous Imagination, Silent Assimilation*. 2014.
7   See the important series: Newearth.

of Knowledge...were from these civilizations. Maybe they were escaping the destruction of their own culture from these parasites and maybe natural disasters, as well. Maybe they spread out and integrated into less advanced cultures to pass on their knowledge and rebuild their world, a struggle they've been having ever since. Maybe this was a back-and-forth that was finally laid to rest with the Reformation and the European Expansion and the Inquisition and Colonialism and the Spanish Conquest. Is it possible that these were all aspects of one campaign? Could it be that something more epic and not so distant was hidden away over that period of time? Could the genii have been put back in the bottle just a few hundred years ago? Is a campaign of this magnitude feasible...cultures we think died out may have been slaughtered then moved into the past. *...maybe this manipulation hasn't happened throughout humanity's time line but humanity's time line has been altered to reflect that it has.* (ie, Zachariah Sitchen's work, which I do not subscribe to8)....the Inquisiton followed by Columbus into North America followed by Cortez in Mexico...could this all be part of the same elite, the same campaign, the same Parasite making sure that their way is the only way, their history is the only history?9 Say it again: all history with the exceptions of the Great Oral Histories, such as the Veda, are lies. Be aware, though, that the United Nations is a Jesuit-run octopus and has recently announced plans to re-locate to India, home of one of the most indestructible and potent oral histories ever: the Vedic Texts. Their aim in my opinion? To take these precious historical records on and destroy them once and for all.

---

8   Zecharia Sitchen a Soviet-born American author of books proposing an explanation for human origins involving ancient astronauts. Sitchin attributes the creation of the ancient Sumerian culture to the Annunaki, which he states was a race of extraterrestrials from a planet called *Nibiru*. He believed this hypothetical planet of Nibiru to be in an elongated, elliptical orbit in the Earth's own Solar System, asserting that Sumerian mythology reflects this. It should be noted that Sitchen believes humanity is a bred slave race.

9   Reprinted with permission. https://www.youtube.com/watch?v=sgje5d5APTA&list=PLJk0yT4erxuSEyHu-0wfUQ0WulbjtWJOu **Carlwood, Greg. Newearth: Basic Principles and Concepts**

11

Quiz: who said, He who controls the past, controls the future? Right, George Orwell. I hope that statement takes on a whole new meaning for the reader now. 10 Point one: the modern chronology is dead wrong.

Most of us think of history as history and have no working idea that there is such a thing as an accepted chronology. We may think in terms of a simple but finite timeline, a tool for discussing a specific series of events. What, then, is a chronology? Chronology (from Latin chronologia, from Ancient Greek χρόνος, chronos, "time"; and -λογία, -logia) is the science of arranging events in their order of occurrence in time. Consider, for example, the use of a timeline or sequence of events."[11] The two parts of a chronology are 'calendar' and 'era'. Chronology is important for many reasons. First, dates, places and events are used to justify historical acts whether it be a war over land or an agreement, the claims of royal persons to thrones and jurisdiction over physical territory, and so forth. Chronologies are used as bases in many sciences. However, the science on which chronology itself is based is astronomy. That is because astronomical events are calculable with mathematical precision especially in terms of cycles or eclipses. These help to locate events in space and time. Hence, chronology really is an extension of astronomy. The methods of physical historical verification such as carbon dating and numismatic verification and dendrition (tree rings), are a back-up to the mathematical precision of the predictable movements of heavenly bodies. There is what is known as a Consensual Chronology, an accepted account of dates, events, places and people. It is on this that we verify historical events. It has been determined over centuries really to be patently incorrect in its present form. This matters because the chronology is used to justify particular social actions.

---

[10] "Who controls the past controls the future; who controls the present controls the past." Ingsoc (Newspeak for English Socialism or the English Socialist Party) is the political ideology of the totalitarian government of Oceania in **George Orwell**'s dystopian novel Nineteen Eighteen-Four.

[11] https://en.wikipedia.org/wiki/Chronology

IVANOWA

The newearth woman, Silvie Ivanowa, a Slav researcher lives in Austria, has demonstrated clearly and visually, that the remnants of the Survivors of the Atlantean Civilization were (are?) among us until just a few centuries ago. She uses the research coming out of Russia extensively although the paths diverge eventually on some important points. The accepted chronology completely ignores this possibility. Instead, many signs of their presence, according to Ivanowa, are attributed to a million and one other things, some plausible and some provably ridiculous. This is what started Ivanowa on her research path.

It is very important for me to note that she is one of the most important people who led me to this episode; someone with whom I have so far only corresponded via email. Silvie Ivanowa has a youtube series, called newearth: the survivors.[12] It is a vast compendium of narrated data, both visual and historical, on history and on the megaliths and so-called ancient artefacts. The first item which came to my attention was her bringing to the world the aerial views of a fellow called Gary Schoneung[13]. Among other things, he showed clearly how the planet is covered with straight lines, some of which seem to be very wide irrigation networks, going on for mile after mile, country after country, continent after continent. These could only have been constructed from above. From there, Silvie moved into the idea that the Survivors of Atlantis may have been on the run from the Parasitic Predator for quite some time.

---

[12]   https://www.youtube.com/user/everhungriescatgang

[13]   http://blog.world-mysteries.com/science/from-the-brink-of-extinction-ruins-of-old-earth/

Many of the anonymously built but spectacular pieces of architecture all over the world are quite likely their work. I have no photo to share of this woman but her deeply important work can be found on youtube and I have included the link in the Recommended Research section, as well.

One of her works is titled, "When the Atlantis and Hyperborea Survivors Wake Up." Well, guess what? We are all waking up. Silvie was certainly one of the first to latch on to Russian mathematician Anatoly Fomenko's work and really make use of it in explanation of the world we simply cannot comprehend because it makes no internal sense to us. Like Sylvie, I have been extremely lucky to be able to pull from non-English sources...in her case Russian and, in my case, German and through Sylvie, Russian. We hear whispers and murmuring from a world thinly veiled or just out of our reach. It is only out of our reach because the Predator has built a hologram around it and in our minds. This hologram means nothing to us really. When we know it is there, it will come down. What stems from her research and that of many, many others could be called The New Chronology Movement. I certainly count myself as part of that movement.

"It is being suggested that the entire historical paradigm that is being taught in schools needs a very serious revision. Probably history is more or less correct for the last 200 years (*I disagree. CSL*) and before that it was heavily edited and the more we dive into this...the more manipulated it gets."[14] This is one point where Fomenko and Ivanowa disagree.

The series on the Survivors is only partially based on Fomenko's work. There are some major differences. Fomenko does not bother with Atlantis or Hyperborea. He says all the mistakes began 1,000 years ago. The fact is an inserted history certainly began then, likely to justify the global ruling elite's claim to territory. However, beyond that Ivanowa disagrees and so do I. It's a yes and no situation. There is simply more to it than that. Fomenko does not touch the history of extreme antiquity at all. In fact, he asserts that we simply

---

[14]   Ivanowa, S. Interview The Higher Side Chats with Greg Carlson. 5 Jan, 2016.

cannot know anything about life before 900 AD. This is the scientist and mathematician talking. However, if it seems that these beings were much closer to us in time than ever before thought, then the history of extreme antiquity simply must be considered. I agree with Ivanowa that there is ample evidence of very advanced culture in our very immediate past.

In the matter of who is responsible, Ivanowa and Fomenko also differ slightly. Ivanowa believes that those responsible for manipulating the chronology in this way are those who have authority over the royal families, first the Jesuits and then perthaps entities of a non-earthly origin. She does not openly equate these with the Archons, however. Ivanokwa believes, since she does, in fact, concentrate on Atlantis and Hyperborea, that there was a cataclysmic event. I certainly have that memory myself and it was a cataclysmic water event. She says some of the Parasites and some of the Atlanteans survived...and the chase was on with the Parasites hunting the Atlanteans to the death over the eons. This is a major theme in her work. The Atlanteans spread their civilization over the globe as they were chased and hunted by the Parasites.

Many will bring up the tried and true testing methods that we have been led to believe are infallible in dating artefacts from history. Please bear in mind something I have already mentioned that most people simply do not know: the verification for historical events is astronomy and its attendant mathematics. All other methods are considered to be back up.[15]

Both Ivanowa and Fomenko address some of the common techniques. For example, we have been led to believe that carbon dating is all we need to verify the time of a piece. However, carbon dating in and of itself is deeply flawed. For one thing, it is absolutely unknown how fast carbon decays. Therefore, using the rate of decay of carbon in a piece is ridiculous as a means of dating. All honest mainstream scientists will say that the accuracy is a few thousand years one way

[15] *This is what is at the base of the Flat Earth Movement. If standard astronomy can be discredited then the proof of the lie goes away. CSL*

or the other. Also, the science used to get results is flawed. Most samples are sent to a single lab with a tag attached proclaiming the results that are expected. This is poor science indeed. Many tools used to locate objects in space and time are calibrated, in fact, to give the results one is looking for. Other forms of dating which have been demonstrated as too flawed to use will be set forth in a section entitled, The Technical Stuff. That gives the reader a choice.

As a matter of incidental importance and fairness, we must take a moment to note here that even in the documents available to scholars which may have both been legitimate and used legitimately, up until a certain time, there would have been the following issues (Fomenko calls this the Principle of Small Distortions):

"IN VARIOUS ANCIENT TEXTS THE WORDS WERE WRITTEN DOWN USING ONLY CONSONANTS, WITHOUT VOWELS. Please see the details in the book by A.T. Fomenko [1v], ch.1:8. The vowels appeared later and pinpointed only one of many possible variants of the reading of the words. First of all it concerns the proper nouns and led to the significant ambiguity in the reading of the old names, geographical names etc. In the old text there was also no breakdown into separate words. Besides there could be confusion between the sounds L and R, F and T, B and V, etc. The Old Slavonic had multiple omissions of vowels and besides, it didn't have the separation into words. The 'Ancient' Egyptian texts were also written with the consonants only. 'The names of the (Egyptian) kings... are given (in the modern literature) in their conditional, ENTIRELY FREEFORM, so called CLASSROOM ... delivery customarily accepted in the textbooks ... These forms often significantly differ from each other and it is not possible to regulate them in any way, as they are all the result of the ARBITRARY READING, which became traditional' [72], p.176. Also 'the Hebrew written language originally had neither vowels, nor any other symbols replacing them... The Books of the Old Testament were written using only consonants' [765], p.155." This comes from Fomenko himself and is an excerpt from a piece called *How It Was in Reality*. [16]

Both Ivanowa and Fomenko also note that for many centuries documents were signed and dated with a small "i" preceding the actual date, which then became seen as a '1.' Therefore, a date written as i576, became 1576. This made sliding an extra 1000 years in even easier. The 'I', by the way, stood for Ieuses, or Jesus. Therefore, to add insult to injury, there were also a couple of absolutely legitimate ways to scramble the timeline and its people, places, and events. There is another, which we will discuss at length later. It is better to be sparing with the drier details and prudent as to how much of a helping one serves to the reader in one go.

In terms of the precise mathematics and statistics that Fomenko and his colleagues used to determine the mistakes in the astronomy and to comb through the chronology to uncover phantom events and dynasties, we can try to outline that here as simply as possible. Should one want to go to the source, and I hope the reader pursues this, the exact methods are outlined extensively in Fomenko's history series, volumes 1-4, which are noted in the Works Cited page.

FOMENKO

Ptolemy is by no means the greatest astronomer of the antiquity, but...the most successful conman in the history of science.

Robert R. Newton, American Astrophysicist, (1919-1991)

Bubble, bubble, toil and trouble...(Macbeth)
A dark cave. (Schools).
Thunder. (Jesuits)
Enter the Three Witches...Past (History), Present (Language), and Future (Media)

---

[16] http://chronologia.org/en/how_it_was/preface.html

17

Meet Anatoly Fomenko, who demonstrates so clearly that something along the lines of 1,000 years in our history has been invented and inserted to justify the global takeover by what amounts to one ruling family. Some say their psychosis is an infection, an Archontic infection. What if they are simply a differe nt species ? We can argue that out after we show

them the door.

Fomenko discovered the problems with the chronology purely by chance as a mathematician. He was researching a physics topic: why the moon had been behaving very oddly in the past. He could not believe that a few hundred years ago, the moon had been rotating in a completely different way. While he was researching, he discovered, of course, that this was not the case. The moon always rotated in the same way but some physicists assumed data for eclipses that came from old Chinese Astronomy books were correct. In fact, the books had been misinterpreted. This suggested that the entire timeline should be different. Historic events placed in time based on the assumption that these books were correct must therefore also be wrong. Fomenko was stunned, as he continued to investigate, just how wrong it all was! He then embarked on the Chronology Project.

It was a modern astronomer and mathematician, Robert Newton, who suggested that the moon itself was 'wrong' for a few centuries. Unfortunately, Newton was a top man at NASA and so his 'science' may well be a cover-up rather than a mistake in viewpoint. It does seem rather ridiculous to assume the moon was wrong and not the old calendar.

Thankfully, Fomenko noted that it was far more likely that the man-made calendar was off than this reliable astral body. Other evidence included: ancient documents were often partially or completely fabricated. This overhaul happened primarily during the Reformation – as the name suggests, Re-Formation. Monks were often asked to 'correct' manuscripts. This is blatantly noted. They corrected the manuscripts to suit the new paradigm into which humanity was being artificially driven. The Reformation was actually bloody and aggressive in spreading this new narrative. In reality, it was an extremely bloody war. Many European nations saw a large percentage of their population wiped out.

Two men in the 20th century can be credited with finally getting this abomination some of the attention it deserves. The first was N.A. Morozov, a mathematician and contemporary of Fomenko. Critically, Mozorov solved a complex celestial mechanics problem which rearranged eclipse dates, many of which were used to date very important historical events, thus throwing the chronology into utter scientifically proved disrepute.

The other was the above mentioned Anatoly Fomenko. First, he discovered and read the work of Mozorov then brought it as a body to the attention of a group of mathemeticians in Moscow who began to establish a scientific and statistic method of studying the Scaligerian chronology thus turning it into a science.

"As a result of application of statistical methods to historical science, A.T. Fomenko discovered a "fiber structure" of our modern "textbook in ancient and medieval history". In such a way we will call a modern chronological tradition in history which is expressed in all our textbooks. It was proved that this "textbook" consist of four more short "textbooks" which speak about the same events, the same historical epochs. These short "textbooks" were then shifted one with respect to other on the time axis and then glued together preserving these shifts. The result is our modern "textbook" which shows the history much longer than it was in reality. To be more precise, we speak here only about a "written" history, i.e., such history which left it's traces in written documents which finally, after their certain evolution, we possess today. Of course before it, there was a long "pre-written" history, but information about it is lost.

History which we in principle could learn about today, starts only in 9-10th cc. "A.D." (i.e., 1100-1200 years ago). And the very name "A.D." attached to the era which we use now, is not correct. New results concerning the problem of reconstruction of real ancient chronology one can find in two last Fomenko's books [4,5] devoted to history and chronology.

An important step to the reconstruction of real ancient chronology was made by publication of the books written by AT Fomenko, VV Kalashnikov (*now deceased, CSL*) and GV Nosovskij. In this book the true date of compilation of a famous ancient scientific manuscript, Ptolemy's "Almagest", was (approximately) determined as a result of statistical analysis of numerical astronomical data in the "Almagest". Traditionally it is assumed that the "Almagest" was compiled not later than in 2nd c. A.D. Ironically, data from the Almagest itself proved that the real date of it's compilation belongs to the time interval from 7th century to 13th century A.D." More on the Almagest can be found in an article at the end of this piece.

Some of the other scholars who tangled with the Scaligerian Chronology were astonishingly well-known and highly regarded scientists; for example, Isaac Newton. Newton had access to more of the original documents than others did because the clean up took place after his time. He was also closer to this original history. Most of these same ancient sources are now missing. He tried to make sense of the 'facts' of history and wrote a

study of ancient history called The Chronology of Ancient Kingdoms
Amended. He was never totally satisfied with it and was revising it at the
time of his death in 1727. Newton said in the Introduction of the book
"...they have made the Antiquities of Greece three or four hundred years
older than the truth." He begins Chapter 1 by saying "All Nations, before
they began to keep exact accounts of Time, have been prone to raise their
Antiquities; and this humour has been promoted, by the Contentions between
Nations about their Originals.[17]

German scholar, Gunnar Heinsahn has taken up this study and
has determined that Sumeria never existed and that the history for
Mesopotamia and Egypt is 2000 years too long due to 'mistakes' in the bible.
In fact, outside the English-speaking world, which is kept in an almost
impenetrable bubble, the old chronology is being aggressively challenged.
Oswald Spengler noted massive problems with the modern chronology.

One of the most recent victims of what he knew was Wilhelm
Kammeyer. Kammeyer, who died in 1959, was a scientist who developed a
method for verifying ancient documents and wrote several books saying that
nearly all the ancient and early mediaeval Western European documents
were either copied (and 'revised') or forged in more recent times. Like many
people who buck the system, he died broken and impoverished because of
his stand on the Chronology.

Also, consider the following: "The phantom time hypothesis is a
historical conspiracy theory advanced by Heribert Illig (born 1947). First
published in 1991, the hypothesis proposes a conspiracy by the Holy Roman
Emporer Otto III, Pope Sylvester II, and possibly the Byzantine Emporer
Constantine VII, to fabricate the Anno Domini dating system
retrospectively, so that it placed them at the special year of AD 1000, and to
rewrite history. Illig believed that this was achieved through the alteration,
misrepresentation, and forgery of documentary and physical evidence.

[17]   http://www.hiddenmysteries.org/conspiracy/history/illusionsofhistory.shtml

According to this scenario, the entire Carolingian period, including the figure of Charlemagen, would be a fabrication, with a "phantom time" of close to three centuries (AD 614 to 911) added to the Early Middle Ages." [18]

During this 'extra' 1,000 years, researchers have been unable to find, it is said, any buildings that can be categorically stated to have been built in that time frame. All progress appeared to have stopped. How many times have we heard that no one can explain the great Dark Ages? Many scientists, including a multitude of mainstream scientists, hold completely different views about history but much like the climate scientists and anti-vaccine scientists and so forth, they and their opinions are kept well away from the public. Most people have no real idea about this. Fomenko believes or at least seems to believe that the extra time was inserted to justify the reign of illegitimate royal families.

One of the most important areas of study for any chronologist appears to be the Roman Empire, whatever that actually turns out to mean. Fomenko sees it as an overlay as does Ivanowa. They interpret in slightly different ways. Rome was right on top of the Holy Roman Empire, for one thing, as well as Troy, with no empty landscape of years between, that seems clear. [19] However, Fomenko sees it thusly: These empires were part of entire dynasties which were laid over each other in history. He discovered these so-called Phantom Dynasties by developing a statistical table called a Form Code. This is discussed later in this text. As has been noted in Ivanowa's section, she believes that nation-states were forced to form when the Survivors had been hunted over time. [20] These were the first so-called Empires and, elegantly, we were trained to fight each other as a method of elimination. Who would that have been then?

---

[18]   https://en.wikipedia.org/wiki/Phantom_time_hypothesis

[19]   Fomenko, A. Chronology I

[20]   I believe it may have been begun with the Battles of Moytura, a subject which will be handled in depth in Episode Two.

Who:

> *"Highly intelligent, indolent and dishonest humanoids invented foolproof ways of gaining riches and almost total power for themselves, and their families. They invented 'Houses' and 'Bloodlines' to project their authority and protect their agenda. One of the many ways they accomplished this was through the manipulation of bicameral records to invent de facto histories, religions, and party politics."* [21]

The man credited with this one-and-only common chronology exclusively in use today is called Joseph Scaliger. The chronology is thus known as the Scaligerian, or Consensual, Chronology. He is often referred to by historians, even those who work on deeply alternative forms of history, as Josephus. Josephus says this and Josephus says that or 'we find in Josephus...' Spelled properly, the way people spelled these sorts of names in Scaliger's time, we would see Iosephus. As noted in an earlier section, this 'I' instead of 'J' becomes very important in the extraneous but oh-so-important details of how our history was so easily misrepresented.

We will meet this man in as in-depth way as we can here. However, before we begin, I would like to make the following statements. The Scaglierian Chronology is the history we have written before us to read, memorize and pass down. All dates and events we consider to be true, proper and right were, in fact, created by two Jesuits, one after the other, using what they claimed were ancient manuscripts. These manuscripts were laboriously copied with the help of Benedictine monks, absolutely notorious as a group for rewriting history, and then all the originals...ALL...have disappeared in various fires.

So, then, who was Joseph Scaliger? Or whom does he seem to have been?

---

[21]   *Ireland, Land of the Pharaohs.* Power, Andrew. 2005

He was a French Jesuit, for one thing. (Although it is more widely accepted that his successor was 'the Jesuit,' the fact is Scaliger spent many years in the household of one of the most notable Masons in France, Louis de Chasteigner). The chronology was created and concluded in a series of works of the 16th and 17th century that began with the works of the man who would become known as Iosephus Iustus Scaliger (1540-1609). Ignatius Loyola created the Order of the Jesuits at about the time Scaliger was born. Thus Scaliger lived in a time when this avaricious, greedy and power-mad group was fresh and newly obsessed with gaining control of every social system. After he died, Scaliger's work was finished by another Jesuit, Dionysius Petavius (Denis Petau, 1583-1652). The new history, once finished, was forced upon the population via military power during the Reformation. The Jesuit-run Inquisition was used, as well, to wipe out the old history and force acceptance of the new history. Once the Prussian Education System was developed and successfully germinated in 1818, the history of the entire global population could be re-spun one nation at a time.

The accepted facts of Scaliger's life are as follows. He was born in Agen, which is in Aquitaine in southwestern France. He was at school at the College of Guienne, in Bordeaux. It was a dangerous time to be at a college as the tinder of the suspicious relationship between the Jesuits, the Christians and the Jews in university arenas in France needed very little spark to burst into flame. It was unsafe to display your Judaism especially or connections to it and the slightest elbow room at the table was all the Jesuits needed to swallow a university whole. The plague sent the boy Iosephus home as evacuations ensued and he spent several years there helping his father with academic pursuits.

By the time he was University of Paris, he spoke Latin, Greek and Hebrew. He began delving into Arabic. It was also at this time that he was introduced to Louis de Chasteigner, the Lord of LaRoche-Posay, certainly well-known as a high Mason, with whom he lived and travelled for the next thirty years. It is written that the Massacre of St. Bartholomew forced Scaliger to flee with the Huguenots to Geneva and there he stayed as a professor until 1574. At that point, he returned to France and lived once again with his mentor.

During the last twenty years of his life, having proved himself as a Latin scholar, he worked on a translation of Eusebius, an incredibly important..they tell us...ancient document upon which Scaglier's chronology rests in large part. Eusebius of Caesaria was a Roman historian and the Father of Church History. Therefore, his information is deeply suspect. Of course, there are other reasons to suspect any history of anyone but in particular those who represented to us as 'the ancient authorities.' It is unclear whether this work is still available in the original. Probably not. It might be actually true to say all of the ancient sources burned, in individual spontaneous fires, within a certain period of time leaving nothing but the copies.

Then, mysteriously, Scaliger was asked to come to Leiden, at first to teach but when he declined, simply to grace the university there with his presence. For this mere habitation, he was paid a handsome sum. It was in 1593 when he arrived in the Netherlands and he never returned to France. At this point, it surfaces in the reading that he was considered to be or considered himself to be a 'Prince of Verona.' He became a veritable social butterfly in Leiden. His reputation as a scholar was at its zenith and his opinion unquestioned. He truly ruled the literary world from his throne in Leiden. This is an interesting turn of events for a man who has spent years studying and mapping out ancient chronologies and writing a 'modern' rendering of classics, including Eusebius.

As can be imagined, he also made many enemies from his place of omnipotence. He surrounded himself with young students who lapped up every word. He was conscious of his power but generally injudicious with its use. Nor was he always right. He trusted much to his memory, which was occasionally treacherous. His amendments, if often valuable, were sometimes absurd. In laying the foundations of a science of ancient chronology he relied sometimes on groundless or even absurd hypotheses. Sometimes he misunderstood the astronomical science of the ancients, and he was no mathematician. In fact, based on what has been written about him it seems reasonable to say that what Scaliger was was cooperative and popular.

His enemies were not merely those he had insulted one way or

another. The results of his method of historical criticism threatened the Catholic controversialists and the authenticity of many of the documents on which they relied. It became an epic battle of the false histories.22 The Jesuits aspired for world domination, as much through being the source of all scholarship and criticism, saw the writings and authority of Scaliger as a formidable barrier to their claims. At least, this is the legend. There is much questionable about Scaliger's history particularly since there was a handsome pay-off at the end. Eventually, the Jesuit faction sought to destroy Scaliger's character, challenging his right to call himself a Prince of Verona and so forth. Scaliger was known to be an irreconcilable Protestant, for whatever that's worth. As long as his intellectual supremacy was unquestioned, the Protestants had the advantage in learning and scholarship. This was a time in which the underhanded jockeying between the Jewish, the Protestant and the Catholic often cost people their lives. By 1607, Jesuit-led attacks resulted in a 400 page book being issued refuting Scaliger's work and challenging his ancestry. This is interesting in that it makes one wonder what the relationship was with the Jesuits given Scaliger's own personal history; his life with high Mason de Chasteigner, his re-writing of the chronology, his reception in Leiden as a Prince of Verona who was showered with money and luxury. Then seemingly, the Jesuits turned on him. We do know most definitely that his successor was, in fact, a Jesuit.

Before we move on to his successor, however, we should ask ourselves, what sorts of chronologies existed prior to Scaliger, who made them and how were they used? What was it that Scaliger actually got hold of?

The question is, was his successor actually his successor? Denis Petau, who styled himself Dionysius Petavius, was a Jesuit and an ecclesiast, also of French origin. He is hailed as the man who took over the chronology from Scaliger and finished it. However, there are some indications that these men were contemporaries. Given the monotonous regularity of concurrent events in the

---

22   My emphasis.

chronology being separated and treated as sequential events, were this to be the case it would

Dionysius Petavius

be unsurprising. In fact, Fomenko believes that three sequential chronologists who went by the name Dionysius may well have been the same man, our man Petau.

Supposedly, Petavius was born in Orlean, France, in 1583. He entered the Jesuit Order as a fully grown man in 1605 having been a successful scholar and lecturer. In 1639, he became a cardinal under Pope Urban VIII. Among his previous writings, Pétau had inserted some masterly dissertations on chronology; in 1627 he brought out his *De doctrina temporum*, and later the *Tabulae chronologicae* (1628, 1629, 1633, 1657). It surpassed Scaliger's *De Emendatione temporum* (Paris, 1583), and prepared the ground for the works of the Benedictines. A summary of it appeared in 1633 (1635, 1641, etc.) under the title of *Rationarium temporum*, of which numerous reprints and translations into French, English, and Italian have been made.[23] One wonders, given the written account of the beating Scaliger took by the Jesuits while alive and the reputation the Benedictines have for rewriting history, what exactly the phrase "...prepared the way for the Benedictines..." actually means. Additionally, the title *Rationarium Temporum*, can only mean on its face, the fracturing of time. To ration is to cut into pieces, as in ration, as in fraction. Pieces of time, indeed, to be moved and placed and replaced at will. Finally, Petavius' main claim to fame seems to be having located (as so many did) the year zero, as in the beginning of Genesis. Bear in mind that experts have located this moment with as much as a five thousand year difference. All ecclesiatically approved chronologies however must be dated from that moment in time, Genesis, Day One.

To reiterate, ancient texts were taken by Scaliger and then Petavius and used to create a chronology which met the approval of the ecclesiatics and the

---

[23]   https://en.wikipedia.org/wiki/Denis_Petau

Pope via the Jesuits. That meant that the chronology would have been changed to conform with the Gregorian calendar at the very least. It meant that all of the ruling families of Europe could point to irrefutable historical evidence of their claim to the thrones of Europe. It meant that the Vatican could point to irrefutable evidence that they had every right to occupy their position of staggering power. It meant that had there been any other cultures on this planet, perhaps responsible for most of the great monuments, art, abandoned cities and so forth, they were in the process of being erased from the general memory. The proof of this lies in the discoveries of a 20th century mathematical genius, followed by another mathemetician and physicist of high position and many of his colleagues in Russia.

However, before we move along, let us consider the French era. Another very prominent scholar in Chronology Studies, Edwin Johnson[24], has put it this way: Christianity was created in the monasteries of 15th century France and the so-called Church Fathers were created then and there. They were not working from 'older texts' because there were no older texts. Before that, there was no church at all. This absolutely falls in line with some of the research that has been coming out of Germany which concludes that most of history before 1400 was completely fabricated and the term AD, *Anno Domini*, simply did not exist before then! "In *The Pauline Epistles* and *The Rise of English Culture* Johnson made the radical claim that the whole of the so-called Dark Ages between 700 and 1400 A. D. had never occurred, but had been invented by Christian writers who created imaginary characters and events. The Church Fathers, the Gospels, St. Paul, the early Christian texts as well as Christianity in general are identified as mere literary creations and attributed to monks (chiefly Benedictines) who drew up the entire Christian mythos in the early 16th century. As one reviewer said, Johnson "undertakes to abolish all English history before the end of the fifteenth century." Johnson contends that before the 'age of publication' and the 'revival of letters' there are no reliable registers and logs, and there is a lack of records and

---

[24]   https://en.wikipedia.org/wiki/Edwin_Johnson_%28historian%29

documents with verifiable dates."[25]

The chronology itself, the Scaligerian Chronology, has been deemed filled with mistakes and fraudulent timelines since Isaac Newton said so. Most don't realize that Newton was a master chronologist, no matter what else he may have been. Meet Anatoly Fomenko and his mathemetic muse...but first, what is a chronology?

"Chronology (from Latin chronologia, from Ancient Greek χρόνος, chronos, "time"; and -λογία, -logia) is the science of arranging events in their order of occurrence in time. Consider, for example, the use of a timeline or sequence of events."[26] The two parts of a chronology are 'calendar' and 'era'. Chronology is important for many reasons. First, dates, places and events are used to justify historical acts whether it be a war over land or an agreement, the claims of royal persons to thrones and jurisdiction over physical territory, and so forth. Chronologies are used as bases in many sciences. However, the science on which chronology itself is based is astronomy. That is because astronomical events are calculable with mathematical precision especially in terms of cycles or eclipses. These help to locate events in space and time. Hence, chronology really is an extension of astronomy. The methods of physical historical verification such as carbon dating (as we have discussed) and numismatic verification and dendrition (tree rings), are a back-up to the mathematical precision of the predictable movements of heavenly bodies. That being the case, it is interesting and imperative to note that a mathemetician named N.A.Morozov discovered an error in the astronomical event time line that was so grave it will inevitably send shock waves throughout the world, scientific and layman alike. This mathematical 'error' was so profound as to indicate quite strongly that there have been periods of historical error to the tune of more than one thousand years!

Some of these mistakes were accidental and had to do with a mirroring of an even as separate events and some were deliberate insertions of timelines and

---

[25] https://en.wikipedia.org/wiki/Edwin_Johnson_%28historian%29
[26] https://en.wikipedia.org/wiki/Chronology

forged documents for reasons of personal gain. Regardless, a new and far more accurate chronology has been constructed, one which places Iesus the Christ (if he lived at all) firmly in the medieval arena.

That subject leads us to the idea of 'era.' We have designations, generally having to do with the accepted birth of Iesus in western countries such as Anno Dominii or Before the Common Era and so forth. We have two distinct calendrical systems which mark eras: the Julian calendar and the Gregorian Calendar. Dates moved attendant to that switch.[27] These calendars were developed and used by two rulers. One allegedly a Roman and the other a Roman Catholic Pope. Both the calendars were developed for the express purpose of furthering the personal aims of these rulers. They are not accurate, they are not unbiased, they are not neutral recordings of dates and events.

So how do we know this? Who focused our wayward attention on something like this? It did start with Isaac Newton. Although it is not well-known today, Newton was a master chronologist. He was the first we know of who pointed out major errors in the chronology. There have been famous scholars since including the prominent historian, Oswald Spengler, who noted the same and maintained this until the very end.

"Sir Isaac Newton occupies a special place among the critics of the Scaliger-Petavius version. He is the author of a number of profound works on chronology wherein he relates his conclusions as to the veracity of (the chronicle)...Newton made a radical revision of the ancient chronology based on natural scientific ideas. (11)

Newton did not amend things nearly as much as the later scholars. However, he moved most of the dates preceding Alexander the Great far closer to us than had been generally accepted. Some of the dates he analyzed pertinent to Egypt, for example, shift forward by 2000 years! Sir Isaac Newton, however, only managed

---

27   In fact, the Gregorian calendar was put into use the very day after the Battle of the Boyne, which occurred on 11 July, a very important masonic and esoteric date. The calendar then moved the date to 12 July. CSL

30

to revise the dates prior to 220 BC and the finding only became public in the last year of his life. Unfortunately, his works were published in France without his consent and so he became the target of the church around 1726.

The situation was examined several times over the centuries, by men of letters and men of academic repute (whom will be mentioned later since they deserve to be mentioned). However, as we step into the period of current revelations, we encounter the renowned Russian mathematician, scientist and encyclopedist Nikolai Alexandrovich (NA) Morozov. He was the first researcher in our time who raised the issue of providing scientific basis for the chronology. Having been locked up in Soviet Russia for his heretical academic undertakings, he was eventually released and became quite well known for his work in astronomy, meteorology, physics and chemistry. He was a Merited Scientist of the Soviet Republic of Russia, a permanent member of *La Societe Astronomique* in France and the British Astronomical Association.[28] In 1907, he published a book called *Revelations in Storm and Tempest* wherein he contradicted Scaliger's conclusions regarding the Apocalypse. In the end, the story would become gut-wrenchingly familiar. The same event was spun out several times and included not as the same events but as separate events which happened in a linear fashion. The same event was dated differently and somehow considered unrelated to another when, in fact, it was the self-same event. The similar works of Isaac Newton and a fellow scholar called Edwin Johnson[29] were all but forgotten by this time. That means the similar conclusions are all the more astonishing. Mozorov found that a radical revision of dates was in order up to at least the 6th Century AD. Unfortunately, he considered the Scaligerian chronology to have been essentially correct, a grave error, as we shall see.

"All in all, one has to state that the precariousness of Scaligerian chronology was mentioned rather explicitly in the scientific works of the 17th –

---

[28] Fomenko, A. *History:Fiction or Science?* Chronology I, p.16
[29] Edwin Johnson (1842-1901) English historian of the 19th century, criticized the Scaligerian chronology severely in his working claiming much of it needed to be truncated drastically.

19th century...(and) the thesis of the global fabrication of ancient texts and artefacts was formulated. Nevertheless, no one, with the exception of Mozorov managed to find a way of constructing a proven version of the correct chronology." [30]

Because the understanding of the timeline of western history is built around the founding of Rome, it is important to present some typical issues with the Scaligerian chronology before we proceed:

1.   Despite the fact that Tarquion the Second had been an adult by the time his father died, and that his reign had started 39 years after that, he was inaugurated as a young lad.

2.   Pythagorus, who had arrived in Italy almost an entire generation after the exile of the kings (around 509 BC?), he is nevertheless supposed to have been a friend of Numa Pompilius. Historians are of the opinion that NP died around 673 BC, at least a century in difference.

3.   The state ambassadors who went to the city of Rome, had conversed with Dionysius the Senior, whose reign started 86 years later...a deviation of about 8 decades.

The Scaligerian construction of the building of Rome is a flimsy construction indeed. These examples are endless. And yet, when scholars quote or refer to experts, it is often with 'Josephus has said...' [31]

Again the question of why so sloppy? Another recent researcher called Momsen, noted that, in fact, the Fall of Troy happened just before the birth of Rome. Scaliger puts 500 years between the two. By and large the history of Rome is based on the works of Titus Livy (born around 59 BC). His first works surfaced about 1469 and were based on a manuscript of unknown origin currently lost. "...the numerical (lies) until (now)...the '500 years' that were arbitrarily placed between the fall of Troy and the building of Rome, phantoms though they were,

---

30   Ibid xxx
31   Ibid p.21

have been filled with a list of ghostly rulers, just like the ones that were widely used by the chronologists of Egypt and Greece...apparently this is the one that brought the 'kings' Aventinius and Tiberinus as well as the Albian clans of the Sylvians, into existance. Their descendants did not miss their opportunity to invent first names and periods of reigning – they even painted portraits for better representation." 32

   Fomenko especially addressed the idea of these so-called 'Phantom Dynasties.' He invented a table, as he did with map comparisons, with the skills he had as a statistician, called a Form Code. A Form Code applied to a chronicle means it can be examined despite any questionable assessments of the chronicler. This Form Code contained 34 items, detailed information about the ruler in question. Gender, life span, duration of reign, cause of death, any wars or natural disasters assumed to have happened during the time, and so forth were on the table. Fomenko applied this over time to several hundred ancient rulers. Individuals could be compared as well as entire dynasties.

   We can compare say, two dynasties. From each we can choose, for example, twenty profile codes of kings who ruled in succession. Fomenko called this a 'flow of form codes.' He compared the first ruler of one dynasty with the first ruler of the other dynasty and so on through time. Many such biographies are very similar so so a few matches would be expected. To compare similar dynasties, Fomenko developed a special factor. If the two dynasties graphed by the factors are virtually identical...and many of them are...then we can reasonably assume we are looking at the same dynasty. Some fairly shocking examples of these can be started with the rule of Jeroboam in the Kingdom of Israel and the rule of Constantine I. In other words, these were likely the same ruler in the same dynasty, not separate rulers in different places. The Kingdom of Judah and the Wedstern Roman Empire would have been the same thing. Charlemagne and Constantine III

---

32   Ibid p. 22

would have been the same person. Henry II and Diocletian would have been the same person. Charles V and Barbarossa would have been the same person. You get the picture. Because different chroniclers were working at different times in different locations often the same ruler-dynasty was presented as someone altogether different when, in fact, it was the same story retold. This added length as well as width to the timeline.33

ROME – addressed in the above text. Additionally...As a nice, digestible slice of the sorts of nonsense and manipulation we are talking about, we can select a few of the more important topics each of these researchers dwell on and try to present the anomolies. At the very least, we can present their discoveries. Fomenko's work will be presented in the section following which discusses Fomenko and his chronological studies. However, Ivanowa has stated:

...that the Roman Empire and other empires were a reflection of the Survivor civilization. When the Parasites got strong enough, boundaries were needed where they had never been needed before and thus we ended up with nation-states. Following that turn in human history, the parasites realized early on that the most elegant way to get rid of them is to trick them into fighting themselves. There is a suggestion that we started warring with each other about 1,000 years ago, if any dating is to be believed. There is a rumour of a female Pope at that time, a Whore of Babylon, who ushered in 1000 years of misery.

From Fomenko's Chronology, a very interesting if long passage:...it is assumed that the Holy Roman Empire of the German nation in the 10th-13th centuries AD was the immediate descendant (read that again) of the 'ancient' Roman Empire, alleged to have occurred in the 6th century according to Scaliger. That is a difference of 4-700 years! One of the discussions that may have precipitated this breach of history was Petrarch's investigation of certain privileges granted by *Nero Caesar to the House of the Austrian Dukes.* For a modern

---

33   Fomenko. Chronicle I. P 275...

historian, the very idea that Nero and the House of the Austrian Dukes were contemporaries, those who commenced their reign in 1273 AD, seems a preposterous one. However, there is much evidence to support this up to and including a well-documented history of gladiator fights which were attended by Johanna of Naples and Andrew of Hungary.

TROY:

Fomenko and others have located Troy in Italy just prior to the beginning of Rome. According to the current chronology, these events are 500 years apart. Rome came right after Troy. Scaliger filled this 500 year space with a list of ghostly rulers just like the ones widely used in Greece and Egypt. It is worth making a list of these phantom rulers as it seems to me something of a smoking gun.

Many Byzantine Historians of the Middle Ages refer to Traoy as an existing medieval town. According to Titus Livy, Troy and the entire Trojan region were located in Italy...he tells us that the surviving Trojans landed in Italy soon after the fall of Troy and that the place of their first landing was also called Troy. Several medieval historians identify Troy as Jerusalem. Imagine how this information would go down in Israel today especially with regard to its many, many apparently false claims on the region.

JERUSALEM

The tangled web of this city, where it may have been and when is worse than any. It is outlined well in Fomenko's work. We can begin by saying that the Catholic Church itself moved the appearance of the Angel Gabriel to Mary to Italy. It has recently celebrated the 600th anniversary of this momentus decision! It has been said to be in the Italian town of Loreto since the 13th century, in fact. None of the archaeological sites in Jerusalem, such as the Wailing Wall, hold up to even the most basic archaeological scrutiny. The discussion of this city, other than to point out that it appears to be overlaid with the 3rd Roman Empire as calculated by Fomenko's dynasty analysis, is a bit beyond the scope of this episode. However, it is highly recommended that the reader do his or her own research as Fomenko's work is readily available.

An evaluation of the comets, in addition, which date the birth of Jesus, places that event squarely in the Middle Ages. All churches agree and admit that no one actually knows the date of Jesus' birth. What they don't say is that the common understanding is off by hundreds and hundreds of years.

EGYPT:

Napoleon wipes Egyptian history clean. Ivanowa suggests it was done with the help of Champollion, ironically the man who discovered the Tabula Rosa, the Clean Slate. They may or may not have known they were being used for. There are even suggestions that a translation manual existed before Napoleon to do with deciphering the hieroglyphs. In fact, there is little difference between Napoleon in Egypt, Columbus in America, and those apparently as of yet anonymous modern Destroyers of Palmyra, the Taliban in Afghanistan, the 'Sunni' Saudi-backed thugs who destroyed the museums in Baghdad after filching everything of import. Ivanowa calls all of this part of the never-ending campaign to erase all evidence of the Survivor culture.

From Fomenko's Chronology, Volume One, we read; When the reader inquires about whether any epochs and historical moments concerning the Pharaohs can be considered to possess a finite chronological assessment, and when his curiosity makes him turn to the tables...he will be surprised...with a large number of opinions on the chronological calculations of the Pharaonic era. The dates of the ascension of Menes, for example, looks like this: six experts assign their estimation of dates to this important event. They range from 5613 BC to 3623 BC. This is a mind-boggling range of 2079 years! The most funadamental research has provided the clear necessity of allowing for simultaneous and parallel reigns. The situation has never improved. French Egyptologists place the dates from Champollion at 5770 BC to Palmer at 2224 BC and so on.

Why move around the cultures in this way? To wipe out evidence of the Survivor culture and a recent time of peaceful co-existence. What does that gain anyone? We if the Movers of Cultures and the Manipulators of time are a Parasitic entity race feeding on the negative emotions of living beings on this planet then war and death are what's for dinner, right? Ivanowa notes, with huge import, that if people became aware of just how recently our freedom was lost, they would be shocked! In fact, we have not been feudal slaves for a thousand or more years. The Middle Ages, the Dark Ages...all an invention. All of this has come about in recent times.

We have already noted a period of time inserted between the fall of Troy and the rise of Rome in which a mysterious Sylvanian clan arose and a dynasty was essentially created and inserted into the chronology. These historical anomolies do seem rife with the sudden rise of attendant 'royal' rulers.

"According to New Chronology, the traditional chronology consists of four overlapping copies of the "true" chronology shifted back in time by significant intervals with some further revisions. Fomenko claims all events and characters conventionally dated earlier than 11th century are fictional, and represent "phantom reflections" of actual Middle Ages events and characters, brought about by intentional or accidental mis-datings of historical documents. Before the invention of printing, accounts of the same events by different eyewitnesses were sometimes retold several times before being written down, then often went through multiple rounds of translating and copyediting. Names were translated, mispronounced and misspelled to the point where they bore little resemblance to originals. According to Fomenko, this led early chronologists to believe or choose to believe that those accounts described different events and even different countries and time periods. Fomenko justifies this approach by the fact that, in many cases, the original documents are simply not available: Fomenko claims that all the history of the ancient world is known to us from manuscripts that date from the 15th century to the 18th century, but describe events that allegedly happened thousands of years before, the originals regrettably and conveniently lost. For example, the oldest extant manuscripts of monumental treatises on Ancient Roman and Greek history, such as *Annals and Histories*, are conventionally dated c. AD 1100, more than a full millennium after the events they describe, and they did not come to scholars' attention until the 15th century. According to Fomenko, the 15th century is probably when these documents were first written."

The Jesuits. Truly the bad fairies. There must be a section on the Jesuits, who are the moving force behind so much of what is wrong and violent and false in this world. I believe I have stated, at least partially, that I had not taken into account the black hand of the Jesuits behind the Prussian Education system. When these beasts were chased out of most countries they hung out in Russia and Prussia, countries where the Pope had little influence at that time (1805-1818). To this day, and now with even an openly Jesuit Pope in the Vatican, they rule from behind, their only goal ultimate control and power.

Today, Fomenko and his team have attempted to make a visual map of the chronology as it has been accepted up to now. The timeline they created is 19 km long! They have begun the task of evaluating each point in time via mathematics, astronomy and statistical probability. Fomenko estimated that the odds of, for example, his dynastic form producing two dynasties that were almost identical but not, in fact, the same dynasty under different names, is 100 billion to 1. Virtually impossible. Please read what another eminent mathematician has written about the Chronology, in part, followed by closing remarks from the author. This analysis includes discussion of other dating methods which can be found well discussed at Fomenko's website or in his books. They would turn the workbook into a textbook and not an episode.

For Another Viewpoint

The following is a quote from an article to be found on Fomenko's website. It contains much of what I have been trying to explain but spun in the words of another. I include it as a matter of interest. This gentleman also covers such territory as astrology, an area I have not covered but which could well prove to be invaluable. I also skimmed over the Council of Nicea to a certain extent. However, in terms of far-flung repercussions, it was one of the worst events in modern history.

Modern Developments

Scaliger's work was attacked from the very beginning, but apart from being subject to fine tuning, it survived unscathed. Historians based their theories on it, and today every student of history takes it for granted. Astronomers all did their best to support it with observational and computational data, and other scholars studied the match between dates and the information that can be gathered from ancient horoscopes (more about them later).

Among the detractors of Scaliger's chronology are a few scientists and mathematicians, such as Isaac Newton and Anatoli Fomenko, but also many cranks, the most famous being Immanuel Velikovsky, who made a fortune from the books he wrote on this topic in the 1950s [1]. The latter give a bad name to anyone who opposes the traditional view, so neither Newton nor Fomenko have been free of harsh criticism. Fomenko, especially, has many opponents, who often find good ammunition against his conclusions. Nevertheless, he and his collaborators introduced new mathematical methods in the modern study of chronology. We will further present some of them, leaving it to the reader to pass judgment about their merit.

The Moon's Acceleration

Understanding the moon's orbit around Earth is a difficult mathematical problem. Isaac Newton was the first to consider it, and it took more than two centuries until the American mathematician George William Hill found a suitable framework in which to address this question. Still, the moon's orbit is not fully explained today, and Fomenko was dealing with some details at the end of the 1970s. He was concerned with the acceleration, D'', of the moon's elongation, which is the angle between the moon and the sun as viewed from Earth. This acceleration D'' is computable from observations, and its past behavior can be determined from records of eclipses. Its values vary between -18 and +2 seconds of arc per century squared. Also, D'' is slightly above zero and almost constant from about 700 BC to AD 500, but it drops significantly for the next five centuries, to settle at around -18 after AD 1000. Unfortunately this variation cannot be explained from gravitation, which requires the graph to be a horizontal line.

Among the other experts in celestial mechanics who attacked this problem was Robert Newton from Johns Hopkins University. In 1979, he published the first volume of a book that considered the issue by looking at historical solar eclipses [11]. Five years later, he came up with a second volume, which approached the problem from the point of view of lunar observations. His conclusion was that the behavior of D'' could be explained only by factoring in some unknown forces [12].

Fomenko found the idea of unknown forces outlandish, so he used his own chronology to redate Robert Newton's astronomical records, which led to the conclusion that D'' was almost constant in time [2]. His result was in agreement with Newtonian gravitation, according to which the rotation of the Earth around its axis slows down when D'' decreases.

Robert Newton either ignored Fomenko's results or never learned about them. For the rest of his life, he continued to present evidence for the unpredictable changes of the moon's acceleration. Among the potential factors that change the values of D'', he suggested the Earth's magnetic force, the tidal friction between water and sea bottoms, the growth of the Earth's core, and the withdrawal of the ice caps, but he offered no computations towards proving their influence on the behavior of D''.

Fomenko and Newton approached the problem from opposite points of view. The former doubted the date of every eclipse, whereas the latter accepted them all, going as far as to disagree with the descriptions of the ancient observers, trusting only a few of the 370 cases he studied: "We have found too many instances of an eclipse that could not possibly have been total but that was so recorded, sometimes in a quite picturesque manner," he wrote in the second volume of his book. Fomenko, instead, trusted the word of the observers, refusing to accept the existence of mysterious forces. A closer look at the data, however, shows that Fomenko's graph after AD 900 is similar to Newton's. In the middle period, for which Newton found a sharp drop of D'', Fomenko obtained results he deemed unreliable. The most ancient period vanished, because he shifted the chronology forward in time.

So, if we ignore the period before AD 900, there is not much difference between the results of Newton and Fomenko. The change of chronology has not led to a straight line starting with antiquity but has only eliminated the data before AD 500 and cast a doubt upon the information between 500 and 900. Newton's results can be interpreted similarly: if we exclude the possibility of mysterious forces, his graph puts traditional ancient and medieval chronology in doubt.

Calendar Reform and the Council of Nicaea

The Christian calendar has its origins in Rome. In 46 BC, Julius Caesar established the length of months at thirty or thirty-one days, except for February, for which he introduced the leap year. Subsequently the emperors Augustus and Constantine the Great slightly amended it.

The solar and the Julian year differ by only a few minutes, but this little discrepancy led to significant errors after enough time passed. Towards the end of the sixteenth century, for instance, the spring equinox fell in early March. In 1582, this anomaly prompted Pope Gregory XIII to issue a papal bull, according to which that year's month of October was shortened by ten days and the day of February 29 was cancelled in the end-of-the-century years, except for years that are multiples of 400.

But Gleb Nosovski, a close collaborator of Anatoli Fomenko, disagreed with the computations that led to Pope Gregory's changes. He specifically referred to the following passage from the papal bull:

Our care was not only to reinstate the equinox in its long ago nominated place from which it has deviated since the Council of Nicaea by approximately ten days, and to return the 14th Moon [full Moon] to its place, from which it has deviated by four and five days, but also to settle such modes and rules according to which future equinoxes and the 14th Moon would never move off their places. . . . Therefore, to return the equinox to its proper place established by the Church fathers of the Council of Nicaea on the 12th day before the April calends [March 21], we prescribe and order relative to October of the current year, 1582, that ten days, from the third day before nonas [October 5] to the eve of the ides [October 14] inclusive, be deleted.

Nosovski found two errors in this quote. The first has to do with the time difference between the full moon and the spring equinox, an interval the bull wants to keep constant. But this cannot be done, because the cycle of full moons and the date of the equinox shift at different rates. Nosovski concluded that this mistake likely belonged to those who wrote the bull, for no astronomer could have fallen into this trap.

The second mistake, however, proves to be essential, and it relates to the determination of the dates of the spring equinox and the full moon. To understand it, we should mention that Scaliger dated the First Council of Nicaea at AD 325. This year is crucial for the accuracy of the Gregorian reform, because the ten-day correction depends on it. Indeed, the Christian calendar has a rigid and a flexible part. The former is the old-style solar Julian system, with its fixed celebrations, whereas the latter is the lunar Easter Book, which determines the variable feasts and festivals of the Christian church. With no exception, all religious services are based on these two systems.

Tradition claims that the difficulty of combining the lunar and the solar calendars has confronted theologians since the second century AD, when the church first celebrated Easter. The Easter Book, canonized by the First Council of Nicaea in AD 325, provides the rules on which day this celebration should occur. But the dating system in the Easter Book is confusing, since the original text of the

Nicaean Creed has not survived. We know how to compute the date of Easter only from the message of Constantine to the bishops who were absent from the council, and this document doesn't ask for Easter to take place after the spring equinox. By about AD 1330, the medieval scholar Matthew Vlastar wrote the following about how to determine the anniversary of Christ's resurrection in the *Collection of Rules of the Holy Fathers of the Church*:

The rule on Easter has two restrictions: not to celebrate together with the Israelites and to celebrate after the spring equinox. Two more were added by necessity: to have the festival after the very first full Moon after the equinox and not on any day but on the first Sunday after the full Moon. All the restrictions except the last one have been kept firmly until now, but now we often change for a later Sunday. We always count two days after the Passover [full Moon] and then turn to the following Sunday. This happened not by ignorance or inability of the Church fathers who confirmed the rules, but because of the lunar motion.

In Vlastar's time, the last condition of Easter was violated: if the first Sunday took place within two days after the full moon, the celebration of Easter was postponed until the next weekend. This change was necessary because of the difference between the real full moon and the one computed in the Easter Book. The error, of which Vlastar knew, is twenty-four hours in 304 years. Therefore the Easter Book must have been written around AD 722. Had Vlastar been aware of the Easter Book's AD 325 canonization, he would have noticed the three-day gap that had accumulated between the dates of the real and the computed full moon in more than 1,000 years. So he either was unaware of the Easter Book or knew the correct date when it was written, which could not be near AD 325.

Nosovski used Gauss's Easter formula to calculate the Julian dates of all spring full moons from the first century AD up to our time and compared them with the Easter dates obtained from the Easter Book. He thus concluded that three of the four conditions imposed by the First Council of Nicaea were violated until 784, whereas Vlastar had noted that "all the restrictions except the last one have been kept firmly until now." Scaliger had no chance of detecting this fault when proposing the year 325, because in the sixteenth century the full moon calculations for the distant past couldn't be performed with high accuracy.

There is another reason against the validity of AD 325: the 532-year periodicity of the Easter dates. The last cycle started in 1941. The previous ones were 1409 to 1940, 877 to 1408, and 345 to 876. So it appears strange that the council met in AD 325 and started the Easter cycle 20 years later.

Therefore Nosovski thought that the First Council of Nicaea had taken place in AD 876 or 877, since the latter is the starting year of the first Easter cycle after AD 784, when Nosovski believed the Easter Book was probably compiled. This conclusion also agreed with his full moon calculations, which showed that the computed and the real full moons occurred on the same day only between AD 700 and 1000. From 1000 on, the real full moons occurred more than a day after the computed ones, whereas before 700 the order was reversed. The years 784 and 877 also matched the traditional claim that about a century had passed between the compilation and the canonization of the Easter Book.

Unfortunately, this conclusion generated no reaction from historians. Nosovski's mathematical reasoning seems plausible, but it would be interesting to know if the historical aspects he invokes hold water.

The *Almagest*, Probabilities, and the Method of Least Squares

The moon's acceleration was only one disagreement between Robert Newton and Anatoly Fomenko. They also strongly differed on the *Almagest*, the most influential astronomy book ever written. Claudius Ptolemy, one of the greatest scientists of antiquity, wrote it in Alexandria during the reign of the Roman emperor Antoninus Pius, traditionally set from AD 138 to 161. Any firm evidence for a different dating of this treatise would affect the chronology of Rome and consequently most ancient history. This opus touches on the main problems of astronomy, from the nature of the universe to lunar and planetary motion, and contains detailed star catalogs and records of eclipses, occultations, and equinoxes, all of which are prone to mathematical dating. The original version of the *Almagest* has been lost, but in its many translations the work has been in circulation since ancient times.

In The *Crime of Claudius Ptolemy* [10], a book published in 1977, Robert Newton accused the ancient astronomer of fabricating evidence. Newton argued that many of the coordinates presented in the *Almagest* as observations are nothing but fraud. Fomenko disagreed, so he took on the task of dating the book.

His first attempt was based on the fact that every star has a proper motion that is unrelated to the apparent one due to precession. The discovery of this phenomenon is attributed to Edmund Halley, who described it at the beginning of the eighteenth century. Ptolemy had also asked if stars moved independently of each other, but he missed the correct answer.

The motion of stars can be detected only by hundreds of years of precise observations of their tangential components. Using the relative positions given in the *Almagest* and comparing them with the present ones, Fomenko wanted to find out when the book had been written. But that goal was not easy to achieve. One hurdle was the use of Ptolemy's catalog for tracing the motion of some stars. If the catalog's dating was incorrect, the computed speeds of these stars were also wrong. Fomenko had, therefore, to trace the history of those determinations and eliminate from his analysis the stars related to the *Almagest*. But the most difficult process was to identify the cataloged stars, a problem that had preoccupied many astronomers starting with the sixteenth century.

In ancient and medieval times the shapes of constellations were not standardized, and their description was often vague. Therefore, telling which star from the catalog corresponds to the one we see in the night sky is difficult. Ptolemy provided positions and magnitudes. For bright objects identification is easier because there are few to choose from, but with faint stars, things get complicated: in the *Almagest* their coordinates, and also their magnitudes, are often incorrect.

Research done on this problem assumed that the observations were made in the second century AD, a fact that influenced the identification of the stars. The outcome changes for different suppositions. This leads to a circular argument. Fortunately, identification is easier for the stars of zodiacal constellations because they have been studied more carefully for astrological purposes and there is more historical information about them. Of the 350 zodiacal stars recorded in the *Almagest*, Fomenko chose to focus on the very fast ones, with an individual motion of at least one arc second per year, because slower objects could have traveled distances that were less than those resulting from Ptolemy's observational errors.

Fomenko then applied the method of least squares. He took the distance between the position of a star as recorded in the *Almagest* and its real position in a given year, as determined by computations. He then summed up the distances for all stars and repeated the procedure for all years within some interval long enough to avoid bias, from 500 BC to AD 1800. Finally, he compared the results and chose the year corresponding to the minimum sum. Estimates for each century pointed out that the only interval in which the errors were smaller than Ptolemy's ten-arc-minute precision was from AD 600 to 1300, with the highest probability around AD 800.

This conclusion depends on several assumptions, and Fomenko checked the reliability of his result. His estimate showed a very small, but nonzero, probability that the *Almagest* had been written outside this interval. With admissible (but unrealistic) changes in the parameters, the interval could have been extended as far back in time as AD 350, a date still two centuries after the traditional dating. The good news was that the outcome didn't change when slightly varying the data. To gain more confidence in this procedure, he also tested star catalogs from the sixteenth and seventeenth centuries, as well as some computer-generated ones. The results proved more than satisfactory: he recovered the known dates within a ten-year margin of error.

The *Almagest* contains other resources, such as occultations and lunar eclipses, phenomena that are prone to independent dating. Fomenko and his collaborators devised methods to check the dates, which then led them to the time when the *Almagest* was written. The estimates they obtained were consistent with the previous dating of the *Almagest* to about AD 800 [3], [4].

So far, historians have ignored these studies, which are published in a mathematics journal that has a reasonably good ranking.

Horoscopes

A horoscope depicts the positions of the sun, the moon, and the planets Mercury, Venus, Mars, Jupiter, and Saturn among the standard twelve zodiacal constellations at a given time. Except for Mercury and Venus, which are never too far from the sun, with a span of three constellations for the former and five for the latter, the other planets may show up anywhere. As a result, there are 3; 732; 480 possible configurations for these celestial bodies. Because of the planets' fast motion, horoscopes change almost daily. They may repeat themselves after hundreds of thousands of years, or as early as within a few decades. The tedious calculations for finding the possible dates of a particular horoscope are easily performed by computers today.

In the 1990s, Fomenko and his collaborators worked on deciphering and dating some Egyptian images, which they interpreted as horoscopes, such as the Denderah stones, the Esna bas-reliefs, the paintings at Athribis, the Petosiris tomb of Dakhla, and the murals found in the burial chambers of the pharaohs Rameses VI and VII. The difficult part was that of finding the correct interpretation of each symbol. Based on these findings, the team obtained mostly dates from the middle ages, results they claimed in support of their shorter chronology.

But these conclusions don't agree with work done in the late 1950s by Otto Neugebauer and Henry Bartlett Van Hoesen, who published a study of some 200 horoscopes, mostly Greek, but also Egyptian and Arabic [8]. All of them occur explicitly, not in symbolic form, so whenever the text is complete, the interpretation is certain. Unlike Fomenko and his team, Neugebauer and Van Hoesen didn't take every horoscope seriously. They found a few impossible configurations, such as one in which Venus opposes the sun, but most are plausible from the astronomical point of view. They also restricted their study to an ancient interval, ignoring possible dates closer to our time. Their results are statistically meaningful: the Greek dates range from 71 BC to AD 621, clustering around AD 100; the Egyptian dates fall between 37 BC and AD 93; and most of the Arabic dates are from around AD 800. Their book provides the necessary information for further investigations, as there are many more unstudied horoscopes in the papyrological literature, which comprises tens of thousands of texts.

Even if all of Fomenko's solutions were correct, the number of cases he has studied is too small to justify drawing any conclusion from them. Historians can easily dismiss them as irrelevant because of the uncertainty surrounding the interpretations of the symbols. Nevertheless, the study of horoscopes is an important method, whose potential has not been exhausted yet.

Empirical-Statistical Methods

One of Fomenko's empirical-statistical methods aims to identify various chronicles that seem different but describe the same historical period, even if they appear in different languages, call their characters differently, and use different geographic names. He started from the premises that a person, deity, country, or city can be known by more than one name: Charlemagne is also known as Carol the Great, God as Allah, Finland as Suomi, and Bratislava as Pressburg. It is reasonable to think that lack of communication allowed name variations to be common in the past, so such chronicles are likely to exist.

Fomenko designed his method as follows. Take two texts describing several historical events that have a relative but not an absolute dating. Collect various data, such as the number of words used to chronicle a period or the number of times a name occurs in a certain interval of time. Then compare the homolog information. If the numbers you obtain are very different, the periods are probably unrelated. If they are close, continue the investigation with the help of various statistical tools. For consistent results, the two chronicles are likely to describe the same events. Tested on specific texts, such as the Russian Supras'l and Nikiforov chronicles, both referring to events occurring in the period AD 850–1256, the method gave similar statistical results.

A related problem is that of ordering several writings that contain many historical characters, some of whom appear in more than one document. For that, divide the texts into generations, i.e., chapters spanning twenty-four to thirty-three years of history. In any given chapter, only names from the past or present show up. Introduce a quantitative measure: compare the occurrence of names from previous generations with those in the investigated chapters and write down the ratios. Since parents are better remembered than grandparents, more distant generations are ideally less frequently mentioned. In the end, order the chronicles so that all mutual frequencies are close to ideal. This principle yielded good results when tested on reliable documents of the past few centuries.

Fomenko applied these methods to the Old and New Testaments. According to tradition, the Bible describes distinct events, except for the well-known overlaps between the four books of Samuel and Kings and the two books of the Chronicles. But Fomenko's conclusion was different. To reach it, he first divided the Scriptures into 218 chapters, one for each generation that occurs from the total of about 2,000 characters. For instance, Genesis was split into seventy-three chapters: Genesis 1–3 (Adam, Eve), Genesis 4:1–4:16 (Cain, Abel), and so on, whereas Exodus formed only one chapter. The Old Testament consisted of parts 1 to 191, and the New Testament consisted of parts 192 to 218. To check the validity of this division, Fomenko tested it on the already-known biblical overlaps and confirmed them easily.

He then ordered all the chapters according to the above principles and concluded that the Old and New Testaments describe interwoven events and are not separated by several centuries, as previously thought. For instance, the Revelation of St. John the Divine, the last book in the Bible, belongs to the New Testament. Placing it anywhere else would look strange at best since everybody is so used to its current position. But Fomenko's frequency analysis suggest that it belongs near the prophecies of the Old Testament. His new ordering moves Revelation into the same period as the books of Isaiah, Jeremiah, Ezekiel, Daniel, Exodus, and Leviticus. Fomenko himself did not find this placement surprising, because St. John's Revelation reminded him of the apocalyptic nature of Daniel's prophecies in the Old Testament.

Can this empirico-statistical analysis change our understanding of the Bible? So far, biblical scholars seem to have ignored Fomenko's conclusions. But it would be good to see studies that either refute these ideas or use them to better understand Christian theology.

The Dating of Maps

Fomenko also came up with a method for dating maps, in which he used the following assumptions. Once an error is corrected on a map, it does not appear on subsequent maps, and all the accurate features are maintained. So, for a region with a long cartographic history, the fewer the number of mistakes a map contains, the more recent the map. Given a sequence of maps where the dates when they were drawn is unknown, one can order them chronologically by mutually comparing them and finding the changes that occur. Many criteria that involve some mathematics must be taken into account, including the type of map (globe, flat); the kind of projection (conical, cylindrical, azimuthal); orientation; the arrangements of poles, equator, and tropics; the representation of climatic zones; and so on.

This idea is known to historians. Sir Flinders Petrie, the father of modern archeology, used a similar (but nonmathematical) technique at the beginning of the twentieth century, after noticing the stylistic differences between the articles of pottery found in various graves. By charting those changes, he determined the relative chronology of the graves.

Applying this method, Fomenko found that cartography developed very slowly. The maps of the third and fourth centuries AD were simple sketches, very different from what they depicted. Then their quality improved, with the occurrence of the first fairly accurate globes and planar maps appearing in the 1500s. But in spite of having Earth's main features present in the latter drawings, their proportions were still poor. Several famous maps attracted Fomenko's attention, such as the globe of Crates, from the second century BC, Tabula Peutingeriana, thought to have originated in the time of the Emperor Augustus (27 BC–AD 14), and one attributed to Claudius Ptolemy in the second century AD. Using his method, Fomenko concluded that all of them were in fact produced about a millennium later.

Disregarding these conclusions for the moment, the principles of Fomenko's method meet the same standards historians apply when dealing with evolution patterns, as Sir Flinders Petrie did in his analysis of pottery. Moreover, from the mathematical point of view, there is nothing wrong with these techniques; they use the standard tools of mathematical statistics, which nobody questions. Therefore, as in the case of applying empirical statistics to texts, this idea seems worth pursuing. But can these methods withstand criticism on other fronts? The discipline that deals with the interpretation of such data is known as applied statistics, and its experts are aware of its traps, such as failing to ensure that the pool of data is relevant or not assessing how many experiments fail. These issues are overlooked in Fomenko's work.

Although he claims to obtain absolute dates, it is doubtful that he can achieve that without relying on non-mathematical results. As in the case of texts, he might be able to order the charts, but how can he tell if the earliest maps are from the third century BC or the ninth century AD? It appears that, in his haste to support his previous astronomical findings, he jumped to conclusions too early, thus risking making a yet unsettled method look weak.

Scientific Methods

Starting with the twentieth century, the progress of physics, chemistry, biology, and other branches of science led to several new dating methods, which established themselves, but not without encountering resistance. Some benefit from mathematical support as well. Among them, the best known are the radiocarbon method, dendrochronology, thermoluminescence, fission tracking, and archeomagnetic dating.

From the mathematical point of view, the radiocarbon method uses a simple linear differential equation that describes radioactive decay. It is physically based on the disintegration of carbon-14, a chemical element with a half-life of about 5,370 years that exists in all living organisms. Once an organism dies, the decay of this element starts, and the method provides the time of death by computing the variable ratio between carbon-14 and the element carbon-12, which is stable, remaining constant in time. In living organisms this ratio is about 10^{-12}.

The radiocarbon method is based on several hypotheses: the concentration of radiocarbon in the atmosphere is constant and hasn't changed throughout history; the proportion of radiocarbon in all living beings is the same as in the atmosphere and independent of location; physical and chemical conditions such as temperature or humidity do not affect the decay of radiocarbon; the dated samples are not contaminated, so the ratio of carbon-14 to carbon-12 is not affected by external factors. These hypotheses were often criticized in the early days of the method, when large errors occurred, mainly because the measuring techniques were not refined enough. But starting with the 1980s, the new accelerator mass spectroscopy technique (which is as different from the original radiocarbon method as digital photography is from film) led to very good measurements that have small approximation errors. The results obtained in this way are often tested with the help of dendrochronology, the science of determining dates from tree rings.

Thermoluminescence is based on the light that is emitted, in addition to the usual glow, when a crystalline material reaches a temperature of about 500o C. When pottery, which contains minerals (feldspars, calcite, quartz) with high emissions, breaks and the shards are buried, the process of building up this energy starts all over again. The quantity of thermoluminescence found in these fragments indicates their age. Instead of decay, as happens with carbon-14, this process is described by a differential equation that expresses growth.

Fission tracking is based on particle physics. If the atoms of an element prone to fission, like uranium, are trapped inside a crystal structure, the released radiation "scratches" the inside of the structure. An electron microscope can detect the marks, whose number provides the age of the sample, according to probability theory. If the material is manufactured glass, the heating used in the production erases previous traces, allowing an evaluation of when the sample was made.

Finally, archeomagnetic dating establishes the age of objects by comparing their magnetic information with changes in Earth's magnetic field. As with all the other dating methods, the techniques used in this approach are continually improving.

As time progresses, the scientific dating methods have a greater impact on historical research, and someday historians might use them more heavily for a critical assessment of traditional chronology.

Closing Remarks

At the end of the sixteenth century, when historical chronology became a science, most mathematical methods used to determine ancient and medieval dates were based on celestial mechanics. Things changed in the twentieth century with the introduction of several scientific dating methods. In parallel, some mathematicians tried new approaches, with some degree of success. These methods provide insight into history but don't seem to be taken very seriously if regarded alone.

Indeed, historians usually take the results of these methods into account only when the conclusions agree with their chronological expectations. In other words, they give priority to traditional chronology over the above scientific and mathematical methods. This attitude is not surprising. After all, they built the traditional chronology with much effort over a significant interval of time. Nevertheless, it is clear that the more distant historical dates go into the past, the less reliable they are. So, next time we hear that Rome was founded in 753 BC, we should take the claim with a grain of salt. We may actually never know for sure

53

exactly when that happened, but we need to hope that the ordering of historical events is correct.

The mathematical methods described above are a first step towards providing historians with more than their original chronological tools and help them keep regarding the past critically. But it is a hasty move to jump to conclusions about the correct dating of ancient events without corroborating many pieces of evidence. Mathematics, however, seems to have infiltrated the study of history, as it did so successfully in other disciplines. After the dust of controversy settles, there is hope that historians, scientists, and mathematicians will together revisit the existing methods and devise new tools, following the same spirit of cooperation that occurs in so many other fields of human endeavor. But we should not expect too much too soon. This is a field in which progress has been slow, and there are no signs that things will take a sudden turn in the near future.

Florin Diacu

Mathematical Methods in the Study of Historical Chronology

Notices of the American Mathematical Society

April 2013, volume 60, Number 4

Pages 441-449

Florin Diacu is professor of mathematics at the Pacific Institute for the Mathematical Sciences and University of Victoria.

Closing remarks by the author follow this particular works cited list, with the author's works cited list following that.

References

- [1] F. Diacu, The Lost Millennium: History's Timetables under Siege, 2nd ed., Johns Hopkins Univ. Press, 2011.

- [2] A. T. Fomenko, The jump of the second derivative of the moon's elongation, Cel. Mech. 25 (1981), 33–40.

- [3] A. T. Fomenko, V. V. Kalashnikov, and G. V. Nosovski, When was Ptolemy's star catalogue in *Almagest* compiled in reality? Statistical analysis, Acta Appl. Math. 17 (1989), 203–229.

- [4] , The dating of Ptolemy's *Almagest* based on the covering of the stars and on lunar eclipses, Acta Appl. Math. 29 (1992), 281–298.

- [5] A. Grafton, Joseph Scaliger: A Study in the History of Classical Scholarship, vol. 2, Historical Chronology, Clarendon Press, Oxford, 1993.

- [6] , A premature autobiography?, unpublished manuscript, 2002.

- [7] D. Hay, Annalists and Historians: Western Historiography from the Eighth to the Eighteenth Centuries, Methuen, London, 1977.

- [8] O. Neugebauer and H. B. Van Hosen, Greek Horoscopes, Amer. Philos. Soc., Philadelphia, 1959.

- [9] I. Newton, The Chronology of Ancient Kingdoms Amended, J. Tonson, J. Osborn, and T. Longman, London, 1728.

- [10] R. Newton, The Crime of Claudius Ptolemy, Johns Hopkins Univ. Press, 1977.

- [11] , The Moon's Acceleration and Its Physical Origin, Vol. 1, As Deduced from Solar Eclipses, Johns Hopkins Univ. Press, 1979.

- [12] , The Moon's Acceleration and Its Physical Origin, Vol. 2, As Deduced from General Lunar Observations, Johns Hopkins Univ. Press, 1984.

- [13] R. L. Reese, S. M. Everett, and E. D. Craun, The origin of the Julian Period: An application of congruences and the Chinese Remainder Theorem, Amer. J. Phys. 49 (1981), 658–661.

- [14] E. M. Reingold and N. Dershowitz, Calendrical Calculations: The Millennium Edition, Cambridge Univ. Press, 2001.

- [15] J. Repcheck, The Man Who Found Time: James Hutton and the Discovery of Earth's Antiquity, Perseus, Cambridge, Mass., 2003.

55

- [16] A. A. Zalyzniak, Linguistics according to A. T. Fomenko, Russian Math. Surveys 55 (2000), 369–404.

It is imperative that we disseminate this information now, using the means we have at our disposal in the internet age. These have not been available until now. The fact is, though, that the Parasite has the same equipment and can and is trying to, I believe, close the gaps so that we have no idea what has happened. Ivanowa has compiled 42 or more videos worth of reasonable evidence that the Survivors of the golden age humanity experienced for most of its existence is in our immediate past! I recommend that, as a significant part of the work the reader takes away from this workbook, these videos and this evidence is examined and let your Imaginations Be Fired!!

Cara St.Louis

Works Cited and Recommended Research

Fomenko, Anatoly T. *History: Fiction or Science Chronology 1, 2, 3 and 4.*

Fomenko, Anatoly T. Various Topics: Medieval, China, Russia and so forth, alas only available in kindle versions and probably not for much longer. (*I am personally trying to make sure I have all the paper editions I can find. CSL)*

Newearth Series: The Survivors. Silvie Ivanowa.
https://www.youtube.com/user/everhungriescatgang

Power, Andrew. *Ireland, Land of the Pharoahs*

St.Louis, Cara. *Dangerous Imagination, Silent Assimilation.*

Williamson, Robin. *A Tale of the Deeds of the Tuatha Dé Danann*
https://www.youtube.com/watch?v=4WB17qv-joc

Schoneung, Gary. *The Ruins of Old Earth Series (no audio) Incorporated into the Newearth series with explanation.*
https://www.youtube.com/watch?v=ExzeKeJQ_lI&list=PLJk0yT4erxuRE86 FDwojIenPk4Ykc2NMy

Fomenko, A. *http://chronologia.org/en/index.html*

Please be aware that there are a few very popular speakers/writers working who have completely pilfered the work of others and are not giving credit where credit is due. Therefore, some of these items may seem familiar. My sources are the original sources. Additionally, I would just like to note that any editing issues fall squarely on the shoulders of both Libre Office Writer and the Ubuntu Operating system, both of which I personally find to be all but useless. When I can afford a new computer and Windows 7, I will get them and the editing will be better. CSL

Made in the USA
Middletown, DE
11 October 2017